A World of Colored Threads

a world of colored threads

by Nance A.K. Stamper

[signature]

Edited by Louisa M.N. Thomason.
Black & white photographs by Jane K. Abrams.
Cover art by Nance A.K. Stamper.

Belleville, Ontario, Canada

A World of Colored Threads

Copyright © 2002, Nance A.K. Stamper

First printing September 2002
Second printing January 2004

All Rights Reserved. No part of this publication may be reproduced, stored in a retrieval system or transmitted in any form or by any means – electronic, mechanical, photocopy, recording or any other – except for brief quotations in printed reviews, without the prior permission of the author.

All Scripture quotations, unless otherwise specified, are from *The Holy Bible, New International Version*. Copyright © 1973, 1978, 1984 International Bible Society. Used by permission of Zondervan Publishing House. All rights reserved.

ISBN: 1-55306-396-1

For more information or
to order additional copies, please contact:

Nance A.K. Stamper
6 Inlet Circle, Palmyra, VA 22963 USA
(434) 589-8859
or Essence Publishing (below)

Essence Publishing is a Christian Book Publisher dedicated to furthering the work of Christ through the written word. *Guardian Books* is an imprint of *Essence Publishing*. For more information, contact:
20 Hanna Court, Belleville, Ontario, Canada K8P 5J2.
Phone: 1-800-238-6376. Fax: (613) 962-3055.
E-mail: publishing@essencegroup.com
Internet: www.essencegroup.com

Printed in Canada
by

Guardian BOOKS

*Dedicated to my mother,
who is worth far more than rubies.
Thank you for buying me my first box of crayons.*

Table of Contents

God Spoke 11
Your Word Is As Water 12
It's A Beautiful Morning 13
Grace 14
Be Still 15
Morning Dance 17
A Home Among The Trees 18
All Things Are Possible 19
Oh, To Be A Tiny Creature! 21
Quietly Covering 22
Believe 23
Hiking 24
Amazed 25

Hide And Seek 27
Golden Bowls Of Incense 28
Awakening 29
Full Of Wonder 31
Adam's Arms 32
Fear 33
A Crown Of Life 35
Exposed & Accepted 36
Not Like Us 37
Christmas 1994 38
Got Jesus? 39
Idols 41
His Return 42
Love Is Our Escort 43
The Most Excellent Way 44
Haiku 44

Eyes Of Love *45*
Share. *45*
Out Of Humility. *47*
Where Your Treasure Is *49*
The Love Of Friends. *50*
Psalm 23:5 . . . . *51*
Holy, Holy, Holy. *53*
The Tapestry *54*
I Love Your Awareness. *55*
You Speak To Me *56*
Far And Near *57*
So Near. *59*
Angelic Lullaby *60*

God Spoke

I praise You that You spoke
and all beauty started;
the trees were created,
the mountains crested,
and the snow capped them.

You spoke
and all creation began;
the bird flew,
the frog jumped,
the lamb stood up,
and the man loved You.

You spoke
and man's senses were awakened;
he felt the warmth of the sun,
tasted the goodness of Your garden,
heard the sweetness in a song,
and saw beauty in the woman.

You spoke
and Your Word composed Your creation then,
and causes me to love You now.
I praise You that You spoke!

Your Word Is As Water

Your Word is as water
To the truths in my heart,
Truths that have been planted by You.
As they are watered,
They grow stronger
And propagate~
Forever sprouting
And flowering new truths.

"...a garden causes seeds to grow..."
(Isaiah 61:11)

It's A Beautiful Morning

I close my eyes and hear the sweet songs of heaven.
I open my heart and my spirit communes with You.
The mornings will be like this morning.
The days will be filled with goodness and not hours.
So for now, I shut myself out of time
And enter into these sweet songs of heaven.

Grace

All I have today, if You don't come,
Is the gull gliding over the shore
And the lazy rolling river.
All I have is the unfolding morning glories
And the folding evening sun.
All I have are sounds of children
And memories of youth.

All I have today, if You don't come for me,
Is the precious steady time of the day that I live in,
The blue expanse the birds live in,
And the fallen stars of the night.
All I have is my sweet love
And his sleepy arms around me.

If You don't come for me today, Lord,
All I have is the pure look in my puppy's eyes,
And my heart to house Your Spirit.
All I have is Your irreplaceable grace
Touching my life.
And today—
This is all I need.

Be Still

It is when the water is still—
Still to the bottom,
That a clear, true reflection of land is seen.

It is when the spirit is still—
Still to the soul,
That a clear, true reflection of the heart is seen.

And when the sun shines brightly
on the surface of the water
Streaming down to its depths,
The glistening of the water is brilliant.

And when the Son shines brightly
on the surface of our lives
Streaming down to our depths,
The glimpse of His glory is grand.

Morning Dance

The dance of leaves in the morning
comes through thin clouds
rising off the lake.
The leaves take their cue
then dance.
Some playfully twirl around.
Others sway side to side,
circling, reeling,
waltzing beautifully~~
And everything else,
even the squirrel,
watches.

A Home Among The Trees

Yellow hearts hang from a branch.
Orange angels fall and dance.
Pink teardrops a hardwood cries.
Fires flame in leaves disguised.

The sun has left its rays in these
Free falling figures from the trees.
The moon then turns bare branches black,
No trace is left of beaten track.

As chill sets in, the stars increase
And snow's a substitute for leaves.
Then willows bud and lilacs bloom
To fill again each branch's room.

Soon summer solstice ushers in
A host of green, a nest of wren,
And one more seasoned holiday
Stirs up applause with every sway.

All Things Are Possible

I've heard that people sometimes see
The inhale-exhale of a tree.
The life within that branches out.
A mighty pulse is seen, they vow.
The rain plays favorite songs for some.
The bark on trees may dance for fun.
I've heard it said.
I've even read
A donkey talked. The sun stood still.
And all was done within His will.

*"Then the LORD opened the donkey's mouth,
and she said to Balaam…" (Numbers 22:28)*

"So the sun stood still, and the moon stopped…" (Joshua 10:13)

Oh, To Be A Tiny Creature!

Oh, to be a tiny creature
Walking through a mimosa bloom,
Searching for a taste of nectar,
Lost amid the pinkish plume.
In a world of colored threads
That streamline to an unseen sky,
I'd frolic through the filaments
And in magenta roll and lie.
"Oh, mimosa bloom," I'd say,
"I long to fetch my love.
The journey, though, may take a day,
So please don't up and blow away!"

Quietly Covering

As the snow falls silently upon the earth,
So Christ's blood falls silently on us ~
Quietly covering our sins
Whitening the darkness in our lives
Gently purifying our hearts
Falling softly from heaven
Each flake unique,
Each drop divine.

Believe

Cast off your fear and guilt, little one.
Cast them to the sea.
Daily, nightly, faithfully
Sink them constantly.

Arise and walk with Me, little one.
I ask you not for strength.
You try so hard to give Me some,
I want your love, my feeble one.

So cling to Me, my small, small child.
Sing to Me, My love.
For you the angels spread their wings,
For you they sing above.

The more you hurt, the more I'll hold.
All the more I'll take your tears.
I want you close in times of need,
I long to keep you near.

I love you when you run to Me.
I even love you when you leave.
So believe the One I've sent to you,
There is such joy when you believe.

"Who is a God like you, who pardons sin and forgives…?
You do not stay angry forever but delight to show mercy.
You will again have compassion on us;
you will tread our sins underfoot
and hurl all our iniquities into the depths of the sea."
(Micah 7:18–19)

"Don't be afraid; just believe." (Mark 5:36)

Hiking

Our struggles don't disappear once we become His children.
We still need to walk through them,
but Jesus holds the burden.
He takes the knapsack,
and we take His hand.

Amazed

You are my Father
and, as I sit on Your lap, You embrace me.
I realize there is nothing that can harm me here.
There is nothing that can touch me more
than Your love.

You are the lover of lost souls
and, when You go out to look for forgotten children,
I work and wait in Your field
with my eager eyes fixed on the hill's horizon~~
waiting for You to return with my siblings.

You are the giver of all that is good
and, as Your hands extend grace-filled gifts,
I gaze upon Your wounds
then look into Your eyes~~
and I am amazed.

Amazed that I will never know Your anger,
but only Your love.
    Amazed that I will never know my death,
    but only my life.
        Amazed that I will never be without You.
            Amazed that I am even in Your presence.

Hide And Seek

The world closes its eyes
and counts down.
I scurry to hide.
In the darkness
I run to the tree
behind the house
and crouch down.

You are there
in the black air,
in the stillness,
as the world comes looking for me
calling my name,
nearing my tree.

Your arms embrace me,
and I stop my shaking.
Your voice whispers songs in my heart,
and I am safe
because You are my hiding place.

You are the One I run to,
crouch behind,
and hide within
when the world comes looking for me.

*"You are my hiding place; you will protect me from trouble
and surround me with songs of deliverance." (Psalm 32:7)*

Golden Bowls Of Incense

Golden bowls of incense,
Prayers from God's own saints
Lined with love, ascend above
The clouds through holy gates.

Golden bowls of scented words,
Thoughts transformed to balm
Pure and pleasing pearls of healing
Turn chaos into calm.

Golden bowls of fragrances,
Clouds of aloes rise
To the throne, by angels blown
Before desirous Eyes.

Golden bowls of incense,
Ornate yet simple love,
Works of art from children's hearts
Accepted through His blood.

*"…they were holding golden bowls full of incense,
which are the prayers of the saints."
(Revelation 5:8)*

Awakening

The baby said:

"I know my God. He's always there for me,
But only for most precious things will I go straight to Thee.
Sometimes there's disappointment or He won't act as I expect,
Yet when I'm really satisfied I'm sure my life's been blessed."

The child said:

"I know my Lord. He died to set me free.
I took Him to my heart and said 'Come walk with me.'
He answers prayers and through the years He's grown to know my ways,
But being known so thoroughly disrupts a lot of days."

The woman says:

"i am my God's. No other can i serve.
He's called me to His holy side and this i don't deserve.
My prayers are praise. My lips confess 'It's He who holds me up,'
For only He is righteousness and only He is love.

So take my hand, Emmanuel, and lead me to be true
That i may never disappoint. Now a woman's here for You."

Full Of Wonder

He tells me,
"Be like a cloud full of water that can't contain itself
 and must pour its rain upon the earth.
 A cloud wanders through the sky looking for dry land~
 filling up again and again and giving itself
 over and over to the thirsty.
 Be like this cloud,
 not puffed up with air, but full of living water."

"Be like a tree rooted in My hands.
 Growing out of Me~
 strong, stretching, green, fruitful, rising up, reaching out,
 rooted in Me,
 taking your life-source from deep within My palm.
 Be like this tree."

"Be like a flower of beauty in the tears of life.
 Turn bitterness to sweetness,
 cruelty to kindness,
 winters to springs.
 Be a flower in the desert so others can see My hope.
 Be like this flower."

"Be like a child
 dancing under the rainy clouds,
 climbing the branches of trees,
 gifting others with flowers
 full of wonder.
 Be like this child."

Adam's Arms

How long did man find joy in Eden?
How long was Eve unstained?
How many days did they commune
Before they felt sin's pain?

How many nights did Adam cry?
How long was Eve to blame?
How could they comfort each one's sigh
When feeling so much shame?

Did Eve find Adam's arms a solace?
Did Adam's strength suffice?
For now their eyes, no longer flawless,
Had paid a blinding price.

Did Eve relive her joy in Eden
When God gave them a son?
Did Adam's heart lay down its burden
When Christ proved Love had won?

Fear

Fear can be so cold—
Shaking, shivering,
Immobilizing.
Placed in Christ's hands
It thaws
And runs off~
Dissipates,
Evaporates.
The warmth,
The heat of His Love
Causes fear
To disappear.

A Crown Of Life

Can sorrow spawn one to be strong?
Can tears be used to unconfuse
your thoughts to why this test arrived?
your questions asked as God seems masked?
Can hope increase within your pleas?
or faith sustain through hours of pain?
Can joy be felt as longings melt?
Can doubt discern what must be learned?

A test so long.
A heart seems torn.

Yet
His eyes you see occasionally,
His hands you feel each time you kneel.
His Son is known,
Your soul has grown.
His promise hear when tests you bear
"A crown of Life for all your strife."

*"Blessed is the man who perseveres under trial,
because when he has stood the test, he will receive
the crown of life that God has promised to those who love him."
(James 1:12)*

Exposed & Accepted

Only here in Your presence am I
so completely known
and then—
so completely loved.

Not Like Us

We think that our Judge is like us—
Thinks like us,
Acts like us,
Decides and even tries like us.
He is not.
He is ahead of us,
Absolutely true to us,
Lovingly above all of us,
Better than the best of us.

So bend your knee and place your trust
In Him,
the Judge of each of us.

*"These things you have done and I kept silent;
you thought I was altogether like you."
(Psalm 50:21)*

Christmas 1994

You came to us and found turmoil.
    We come to You and find calm.
You came to us and found hatred.
    We come to You and find Love.
You came to us and found dissension and strife.
    We come to You and find harmony and accord.
You came to us and found Your death.
    We come to You and find our life.
You came to us one cold, dark night and found poverty.
    We come to You in the warmth of Your Light and find riches.

"Thanks be to God for his indescribable gift!"
(2 Corinthians 9:15)

Got Jesus?

Complaining, angry, demanding, selfish, spoiled, ungrateful, unforgiving.

I still think that I need to get better.
I need to get Jesus, that is what I need.
My sin is so deep.
If it was not, if it was shallow,
then it would not have taken the perfect life
of God's Son to put it to death.   The only Son God ever had.

If my sin was shallow,
a goat would suffice
or a bird,
perhaps a pigeon.
But it is not shallow.   It is quite deep.

It is deeper than I dare think or know,
but
God's Love for me is deeper still.
Deeper and wider and higher and bigger
and no, I don't need to get better,   I need to get Jesus.

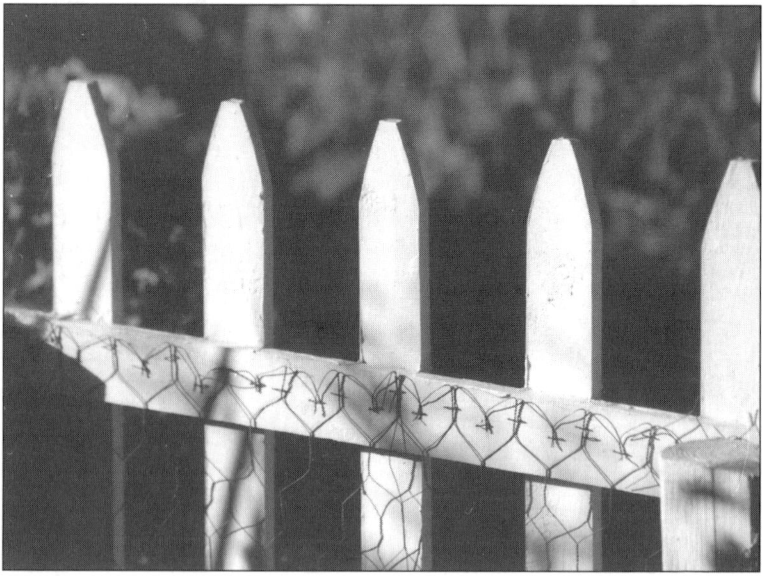

Idols

Idols have always
and will always
be small.
They do not possess the freedom we seek.
They are two-headed—
heavy & hollow—
Ultimately graceless.

*"Those who cling to worthless idols forfeit
the grace that could be theirs."
(Jonah 2:8)*

His Return

Will You come on the sunset
Or come on the rise?
Will You peel back the nighttime
With the light in Your eyes?

Will You favor the moonlight
Or favor the sun?
Will You descend on the Sabbath
And dance when You come?

Will my house be in order
And my heart be in praise?
Will my hands be in labor
Or in worshiping raised?

Will the bluebirds so precious
Be quiet in nest?
Or in sensing Your coming
Sing out their best?

Will Your presence split darkness
And Your essence perfume?
When all mansions are ready
And You come as our Groom?

Love Is Our Escort

It is love that wins us over,
Which brings You to us
And then us to You.
Why is it not wisdom?

No.
It is love that touches us
In the deepest way
And causes the core of our hearts to melt.
Why is it not beauty?
Why is it not power?
Why is it not knowledge?

It is love!
Yes!
You have chosen to draw us to Yourself.
You have made us so that our response to love
Is the most meaningful,
The most magnetic,
And the most excellent.

The Most Excellent Way

The only things that are going to last from this life,
That are going to be taken with us into eternity,
Are those things done in love.
Love's deeds are all that will endure.
Love is all that will last
In God's eyes and in the Kingdom.

"And now I will show you the most excellent way."
(1 Corinthians 12:31)

Haiku

I know I don't love
You near enough as I should
I ask that I would

Eyes Of Love

Make my eyes as Your eyes
So I may see with the eyes of Love
And look at others not with
Preconceived stories,
Critical suggestions,
Nor judgmental conclusions,
But with eyes of Love,
Your Eyes,
Eyes from above.

Share

There is nothing that can strengthen a relationship more
than sharing the love of Jesus.
And there is nothing that can restrain it more
than neglecting that very same love.

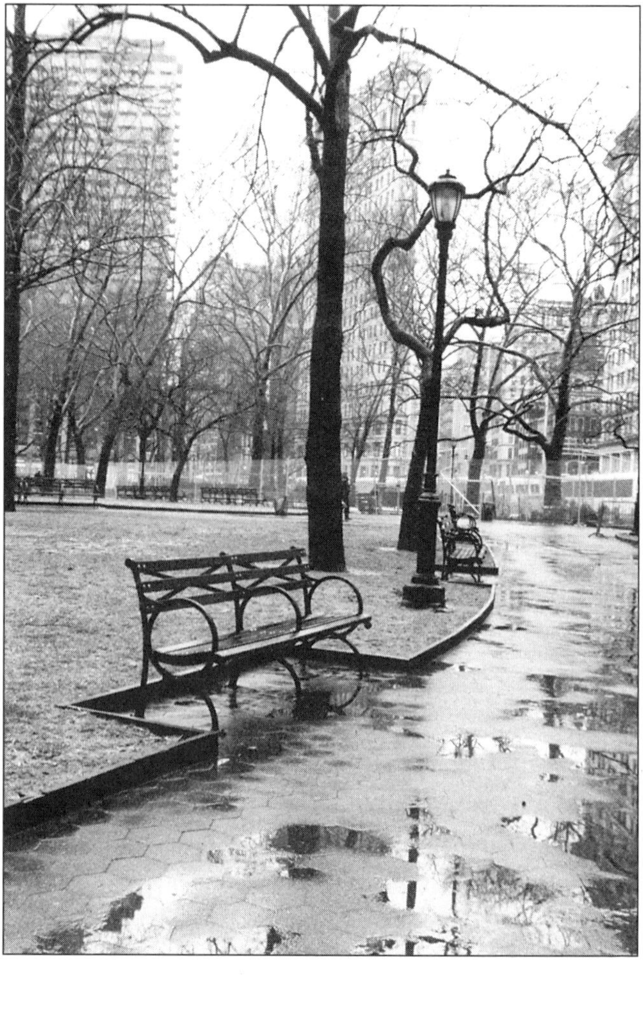

Out Of Humility

I must love out of my humility;
Out of what I know
and what I do not know.
Out of what I see
and what I do not see.
I must love not only in what I say,
but in what I think.
I must love not only those that are easy to love,
but those hard to love.
My love and my humility must walk together.
My pride must be left behind,
Far, far behind.

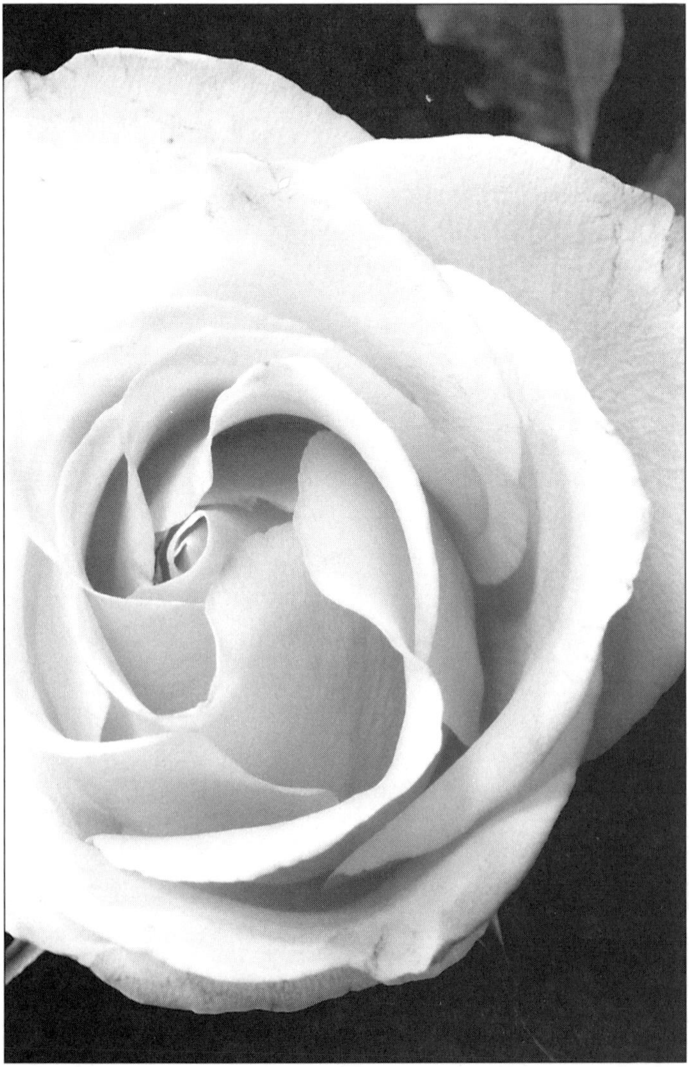

Where Your Treasure Is

It is good to pursue life.
It is better to pursue God.
For in that pursuit,
You find eternity waiting.

It is good to strive for holiness.
It is better to strive for Jesus.
For in that striving,
Sanctification comes silently.

And it is oh so good to look for love,
But it is better yet to give
The love you first were given.
For in that giving,
We are shown the Treasure.

The Love Of Friends

Sometimes the butterfly's wing is broken
And he needs more than prayer.
Sometimes he needs words fitly spoken
To get him in the air.
Yet, even then, upon the ground he'll lie and not take flight.
Even then, he'll hear a different sound and fear his plight.
For words and prayers don't always mend the wings that make us fly.
Now and then the love of friends
Returns us to the sky.

Psalm 23:5

Your goodness overwhelms me;
Fills me up completely.
And yet You continually add
To what I believe to be full.

"...my cup overflows." (Psalm 23:5)

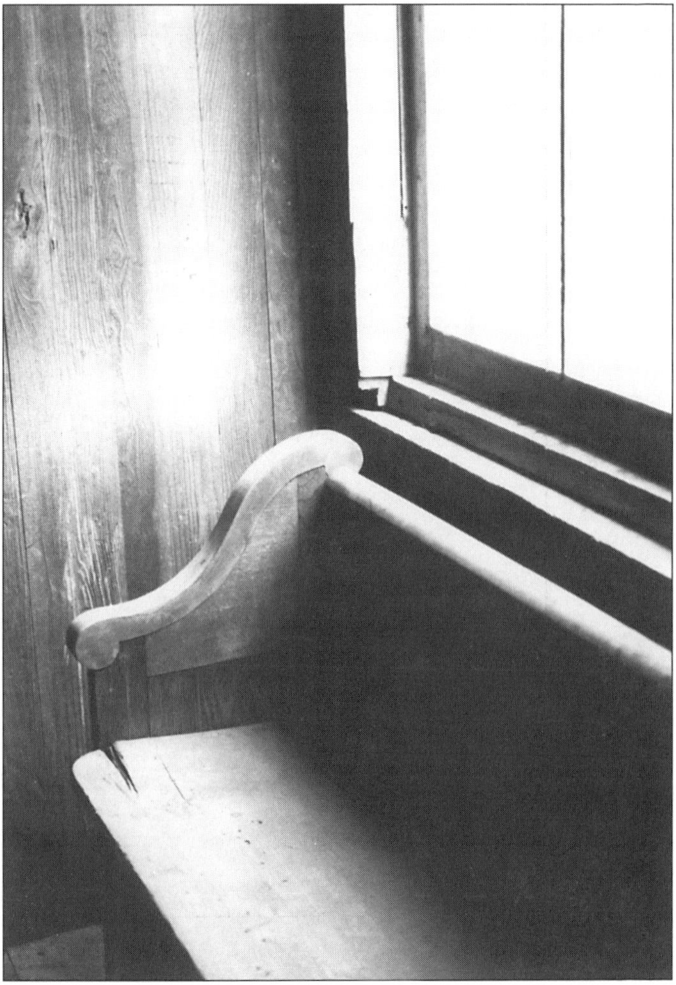

Holy, Holy, Holy

Holy is too fragile to be held within my hands,
Too sacred to be grasped by my mind,
Too precious for words from my lips,
And O!! so incredibly rich when it falls upon my ears.
Holy, Holy, Holy.

"...holy is his name."
(Luke 1:49)

The Tapestry

He weaves and interweaves,
pulls, cuts off,
knots, tears out,
and reweaves;
He designs, creates,
blends, contrasts, complements,
outlines,
ties together, separates,
hides loose ends—
observes,
smiles,
continues…

I Love Your Awareness

I love Your awareness.
It is never careless.
As if I were the only one
To touch Your ears with prayer.

*"Yet the L*ORD *longs to be gracious to you; he rises
to show you compassion. For the L*ORD *is a God of justice.
Blessed are all who wait for him!"
(Isaiah 30:18)*

You Speak To Me

You speak to me, yet my ears have never heard Your voice.
You show me who You are, yet Your form is hidden.
You allow me to feel You, but I have not touched You.
I can love You, but cannot kiss You.

I say I understand, yet I understand very little.

Far And Near

When the simple truths of God are revealed for what they are,
Simplicity departs
and we are left with a sense of God's profundity.
When far-reaching mysteries are revealed for what they are,
Simplicity appears
and we discover an accessible God.

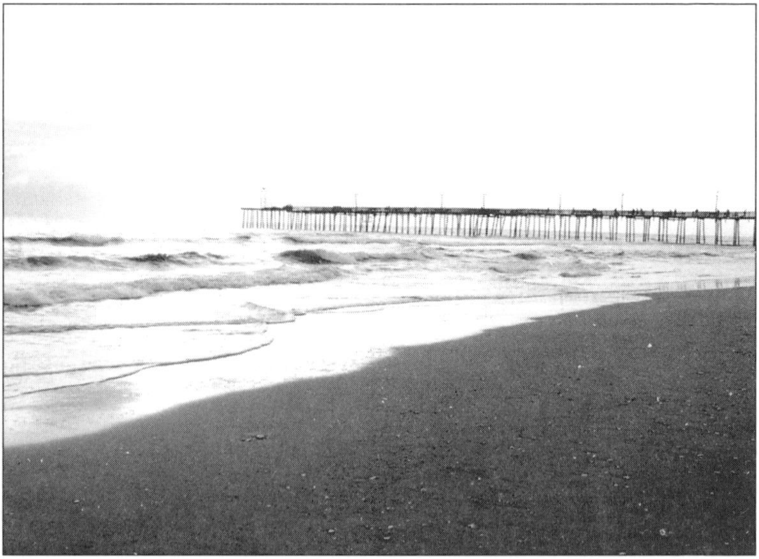

So Near

Who are You that You are so personal?
To know the thoughts in my heart,
And the secrets in my books?
You,
Who names each star,
Who twirls the earth,
Who knows the very depths of the seas.
Who are You
That You know all men so personally—
Especially me?

*"When I consider your heavens, the work of your fingers,
the moon and the stars, which you have set in place,
what is man that you are mindful of him...?" (Psalm 8:3–4)*

Angelic Lullaby

Sweet sleep I bid at angels' feet.
Sweet sleep, their breath upon your cheek.
Let cherubim cloud o'er your head
And put your restless thoughts to bed.
For angels speak in whispers fine,
They weave sweet dreams, weave dreams divine.
They'll cause a weary mind to know
His peace again in morning's glow.
So sleep I bid at angels' feet,
Sweet breath of angels on your cheek.

*"For he will command his angels concerning you
to guard you in all your ways…"
(Psalm 91:11)*